STOP TWEETING BORING SH*T

STOP Tweeting BORING SH*T

THE NEW RULES ⚡ OF WORK ⚡

by DIVISION OF LABOR

CHRONICLE BOOKS
SAN FRANCISCO

Library of Congress Cataloging-in-Publication Data

Stop Tweeting Boring Sh*t : the New Rules of Work / by Division of Labor.
   pages cm
   ISBN 978-1-4521-1825-3
1. Work—Humor. 2. Office practice—Humor. 3. Employee handbooks—Humor.
   PN6231.W64 4 S76 2013
   818'.602—dc23

2012049299

Manufactured in China

Book design by Neil Egan
Additional design and typesetting by Liam Flanagan and Daniel Triassi
Original posters designed by Division of Labor
Additional posters designed by Neil Egan

10 9 8 7 6 5 4 3 2 1

Chronicle Books LLC
680 Second Street
San Francisco, California 94107
www.chroniclebooks.com

THIS BOOK BELONGS TO:

The above person is a dedicated member of today's workforce. And if you steal this book, they will be unable to navigate the sometimes confusing world of the modern workplace and they'll end up unemployed and destitute. So why not steal a stapler or a couple of those big black binder clips instead? No one really cares about those. Thanks.

CONTENTS

CONTENTS

CHAPTER 1

WELCOME TO THE NEW WORKPLACE

OR,

NOTHING YOU LEARNED IN COLLEGE WILL HELP YOU HERE, BUT YOU STILL HAVE TO PAY BACK YOUR STUDENT LOANS.

The typical office is undergoing dramatic changes as employees embrace new technology and find more ways to waste time and avoid responsibility. Startups run by socially awkward twenty-year-olds with more money than the state of Rhode Island are also contributing to the disruption of the modern workplace. This guide is here to help you navigate the new office politics that sometimes feel more like high school than the engines of our economy.

For those of you starting a new job, you will still receive a cumbersome three-ring binder from the Human Resources department outlining the rules and guidelines of your new workplace. But all of it was written by lawyers who are protecting the company in the event that you slip on the kitchen floor and hit your head while microwaving oatmeal or in case you get felt-up in the parking garage by a guy wearing driving gloves and a beret.

Please be advised, the rules in the three-ring binder aren't your guide to happiness on the job and they won't help you get ahead in this world. Though they might help you find the phone number for your 401k administrator or the details of your dental plan. The contents of this book, on the other hand, can be quite helpful. And if you adopt some of the thoughts as your own and make it seem like you came up with them, people will think you're funny and might want to have drinks with you and then have sex with you.

Throughout this book you'll find facts, insights and random observations that seem to ring true. And we believe this because a lot of people have come up to us and said, "Oh my god, that is *so* funny! And so true!" We've broken this book into chapters because that's what you do when you write a book. We also broke it into chapters because the folks at Chronicle Books said it needed to be longer than we originally wrote it. We also bumped up the point size of the letters which is something you've probably done before, like, in college when the professor said the paper had to be twenty pages and you only had seventeen.

Some of the rules contained in this book are less like rules and more like guidelines. And depending on what you do for a living and whether or not you wear pleated slacks, you may find them funny or you may find them not funny at all. If it's the latter, please give this book as a gift to your children.

That should be enough of an introduction for you to get an idea of what's coming. If you're still expecting some kind of self-help book that will give you real rules and guidance for your job, let us be clear: this book will not.

WE NOW PROUDLY PRESENT

THE NEW

RULES OF WORK

Workers should avoid direct confrontation with coworkers and should instead compose long rambling diatribes ending with lots of exclamation points, sent out late at night, signifying long hours of dedication and/or alcohol-induced insomnia.

IF YOU DON'T HAVE SOMETHING NICE TO SAY, EMAIL IT

№ **2**

Employees who never make decisions cannot be held accountable for matters delegated. You may continue to quietly pass judgment on others while washing your hands of anything that doesn't work out for the best.

THE MORE YOU DELEGATE THE LESS YOU CAN BE BLAMED FOR

№ 3

Workers should take note from startup founders who better resemble homeless men than captains of industry: Those dressed like they're going to rob a liquor store may actually be your venture capital money.

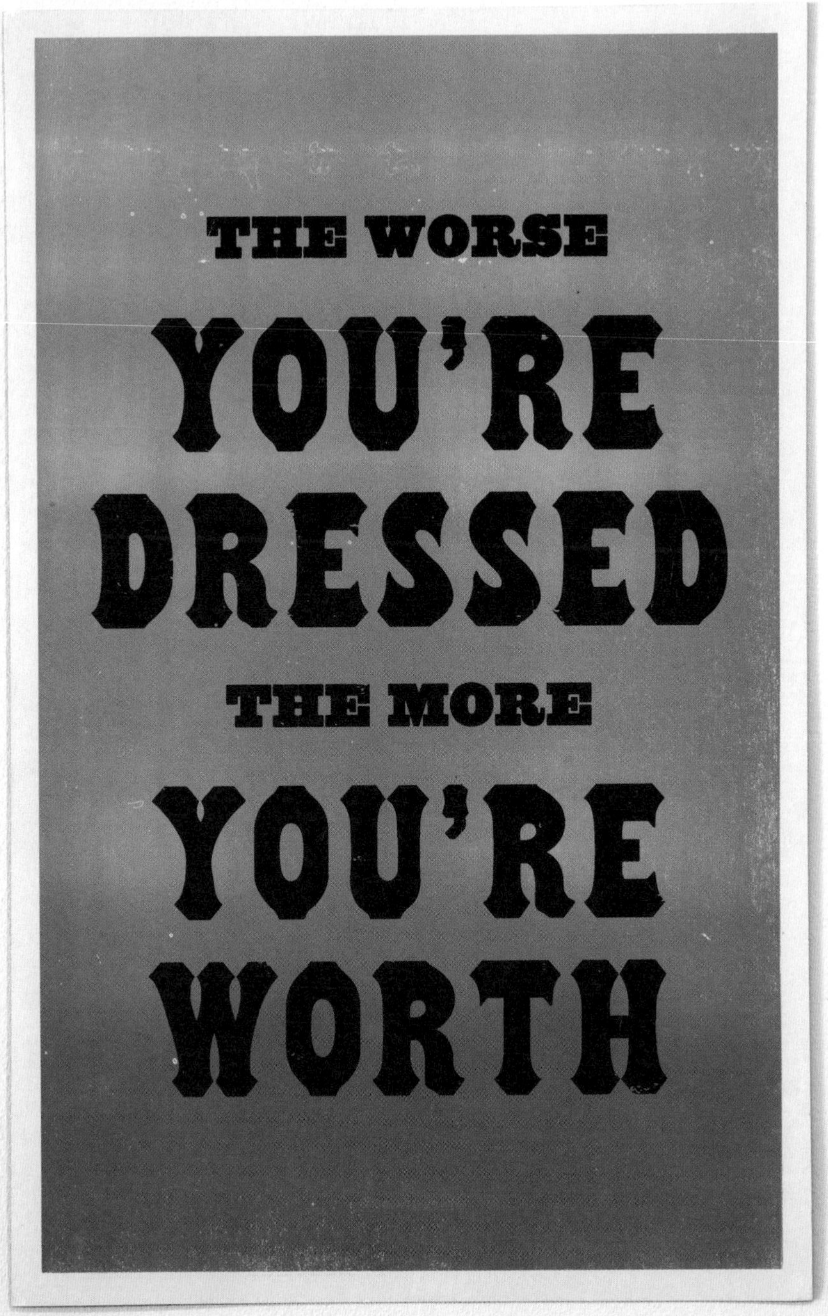
THE WORSE
YOU'RE
DRESSED
THE MORE
YOU'RE
WORTH

CONVICTION WITH SAYING IT

No 4

DOES NOT MAKE IT TRUE

Nº **5**

Before engaging in sexual activity with a coworker, employees should consider whether a fling with a hot twenty-four-year-old sporting a tribal tattoo is worth losing the house and kids over.

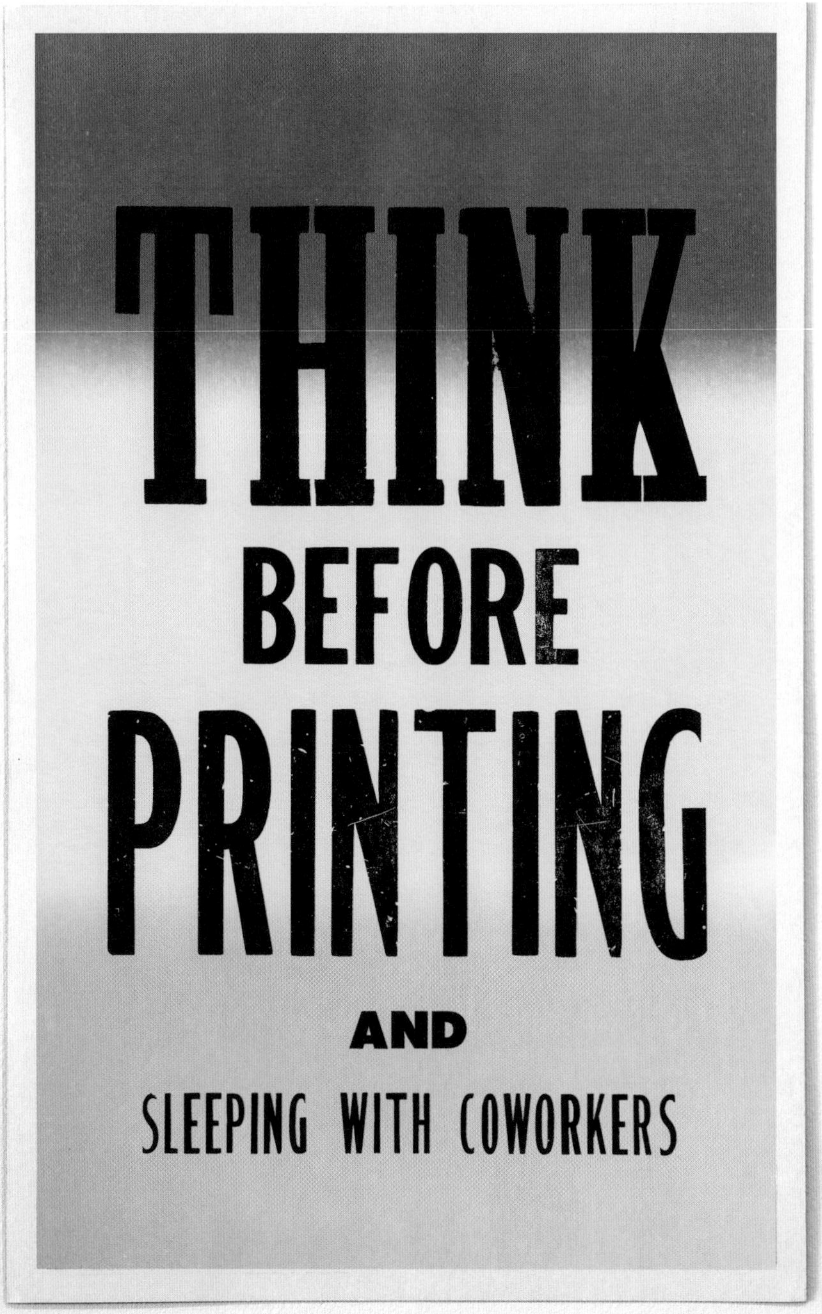
THINK
BEFORE
PRINTING
AND
SLEEPING WITH COWORKERS

Employees who believe that money cannot buy happiness are invited to donate their paycheck to the charity of their choice or just forgo it altogether. Venture capital from Andreessen Horowitz, Sequoia Capital, Greylock Partners, or Google Ventures not only buys happiness, it buys office space, computers, those cool Aeron chairs, and employees to code and get you coffee. And if you've ever seen your company bottom line go from zero to 5 million while sitting in a new Aeron chair and having someone bring you coffee, you've most likely, been smiling.

YC MONEY

$ CAN INDEED $

BUY

HAPPINESS

WRITE THE CODE

SELL THE CODE

REPEAT

CHAPTER 2

TECHNOLOGY AND THE WORKPLACE

OR,

HOW SPELLCHECK HAS BEEN SAVING YOUR ASS FOR YEARS.

The only spot in the workplace that technology hasn't invaded yet is the microwave. No one has invented a technology that can prevent your idiot coworkers from burning the goddamn popcorn and making the entire office smell like feline sweat mixed with vinegar and motor oil.

Burnt popcorn smell is horrible. And it would really be great if there was an app or platform or a few lines of code that could solve this little problem.

The "Popcorn" button was a nice try, but it works about as well as that sign Glenda from Accounting hung up that said, "Please don't burn the popcorn."

Besides the popcorn issue, smartphones have taken care of the virtual work problem. And video conferencing eliminates travel, while GPS tracking lets you know when your sales rep is really just napping in the park.

But the biggest thing that technology has done for the workplace is to make the IT guy king. No, not king. The IT guy at the office is a god. He doesn't need to shower or dress well, and he can pretty much smell like cheese all the time.

But he can still walk in the CEO's office at any time with his ironic Space Invaders T-shirt under his button down and just start rummaging through whatever he wants and the boss is like, "Thank you so much, Ben. Can you come by my house this weekend and help me with my Xbox?"

Then he hits restart, reminds the boss to do updates, and floats out with little wings on his back.

But really, when you think about it, what technology has done for the workplace is eliminate all that irritating work stuff. You don't really have to work at all anymore. You can just look up pictures of ex-boyfriends on Facebook and retweet stuff from HuffPost all day. The only hard part is coming up with interesting comments for your Instagram feed.

In the end, the economy will still go up and down like a yo-yo and all the technology in the world won't help. And just because all my music is in the cloud and I can access my entire office from my phone does not prevent me from making bad decisions, having horrible judgment, or exhibiting lousy taste.

Technology is awesome, but it's not better than a funny story, a night out with friends, or an orgasm.

Which is something to keep in mind. Or not.

Nº 8

New employees should be aware that most pertinent information about your company is available online. Including previous felony arrests of board members and embarrassing memos written by knuckleheads you work for.

PLEASE

DON'T ASK FOR HELP
UNTIL YOU'VE GOOGLED IT

- THE MANAGEMENT -

Nº 9

Workers should refrain from hitting "reply all" and remember that no one on any office email system has ever said, "I'm so glad I sent my anger-fueled rant to the whole office! It really helped my career!"

NOTHING GOOD

COMES FROM

HITTING

"REPLY ALL"

RESEARCH
RESEARCH
PROVES

RESEARCH WORKS

No. 11

(Also note: Executive assistants know the difference between $10 hotel movies and $15 hotel movies.)

Nº 12

Any worker looking for approval on a matter from their legal department should be advised that the answer is always, "no" or some form of the word "no," including but not limited to "probably not a good idea," "hell no, stupid," and "I won't tell anyone we had this conversation."

IT'S NOT A
GOOD IDEA
UNLESS THE
LAWYERS
SAY SO

Those workers not fired in the last economic downturn should also note the sub-rule: "If you haven't been fired yet, it's probably because you're not making enough money."

NOT GETTING FIRED IS THE NEW PROMOTION

I DON'T HAVE

TIME

I DON'T GIVE A SHIT

COMMUNICATION AND THE WORKPLACE

OR,

HOW CUBICLES AND CONFERENCE CALLS DON'T MIX.

For the most part, workers are bad at communicating. Hookers and beer vendors are the exception. They rarely mince words. It's always clear what they're selling and what the buyer can expect. But it's pretty much downhill from there.

More problems are created in the workplace because of poor communication than any other reason. (We have no idea if that's actually true. But it sounds true and that's an important part of communication.)

Workers often don't say what they're thinking. Or worse, they do say what they're thinking. Or even worse, they say what they're thinking but have no idea what they're talking about.

Workers often lie when they should be honest, and are honest when they should shut the hell up, and most don't listen very well, but love to hear themselves talk.

Jargon is a great equalizer in the workplace. It makes people feel comfortable not really saying anything. People spew jargon constantly. If "jargon diarrhea" isn't already a piece of jargon, it should be. Let's see how many pieces of jargon we can put in one sentence. Ready?

At the end of the day, we'll need to circle back and check the temperature in the room to ensure we're using best practices on our action items.

How many times do we hear about the guy who hit "Reply All" without realizing his boss had been BCCed? Or the mute button on the conference call that didn't work while you were bitching about the client? Or the Facebook post that sure seemed funny at the time, but got decidedly less funny once HR found out about it.

The truth about communications is that we all did it a lot better before we started learning things and acting like adults. If more people in the workplace spoke like your average four-year-old, things would be a whole lot easier. Four-year-olds speak the truth: "This meeting is boring." "That client is mean." "Nobody likes your PowerPoint deck, Dave."

If you say nice things, people like you. If you listen to people, they love you. If you're passionate about your beliefs, you can sell anything. And if you motivate people with your words, you can be president. Sad thing is, the same rules apply to dictatorships, so please use your communication skills for good and not evil.

№ 15

Miranda Warning 2.0: You have the right to remain silent. If you give up that right and post comments that "seemed funny at the time," you will be the target of ridicule until someone else within your social network does something worse.

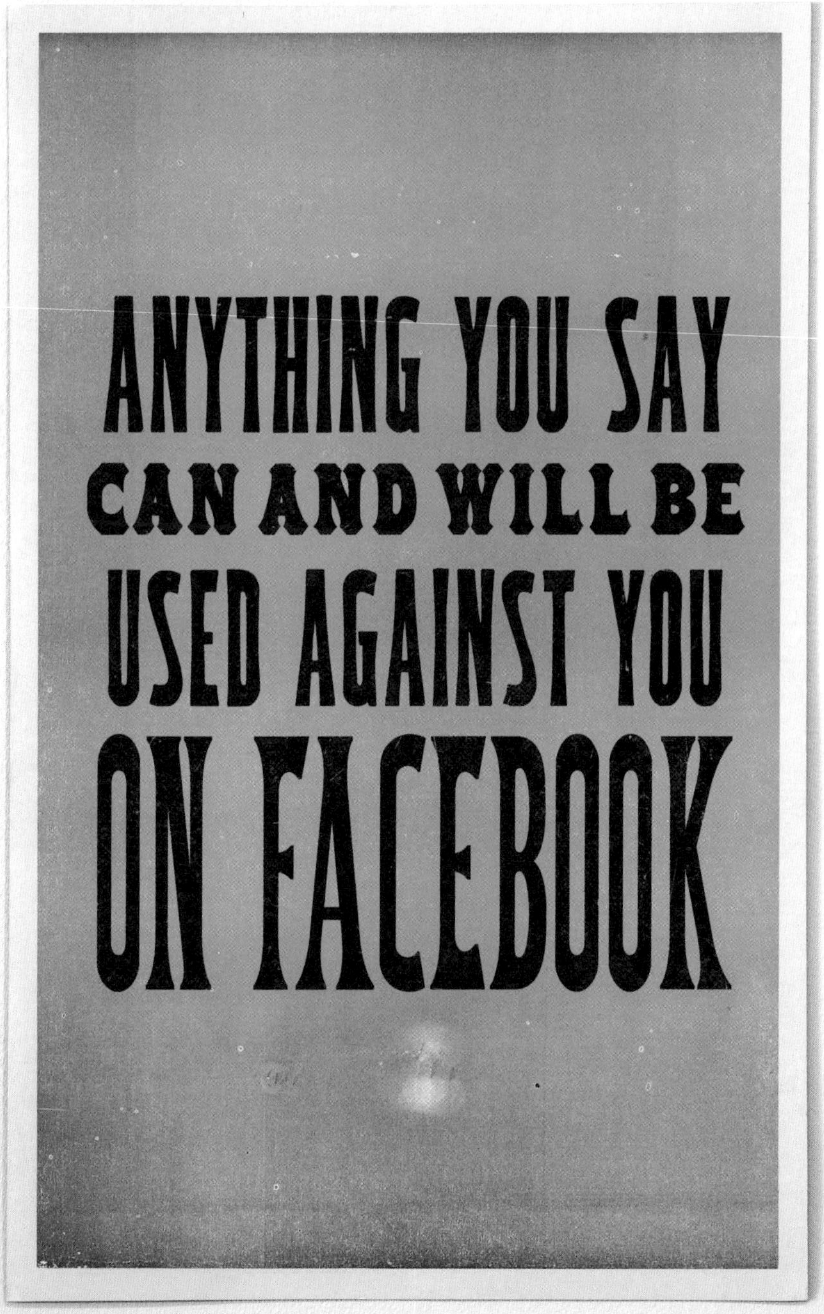
ANYTHING YOU SAY
CAN AND WILL BE
USED AGAINST YOU
ON FACEBOOK

№ 16

Seriously. Stop it. You know who you are.

"EMPLOYEES" USING "AIR QUOTES" WILL BE "BEATEN"

Nº 17

*And irregardless of what you believe, "irregardless" is not a word either. Sorry.

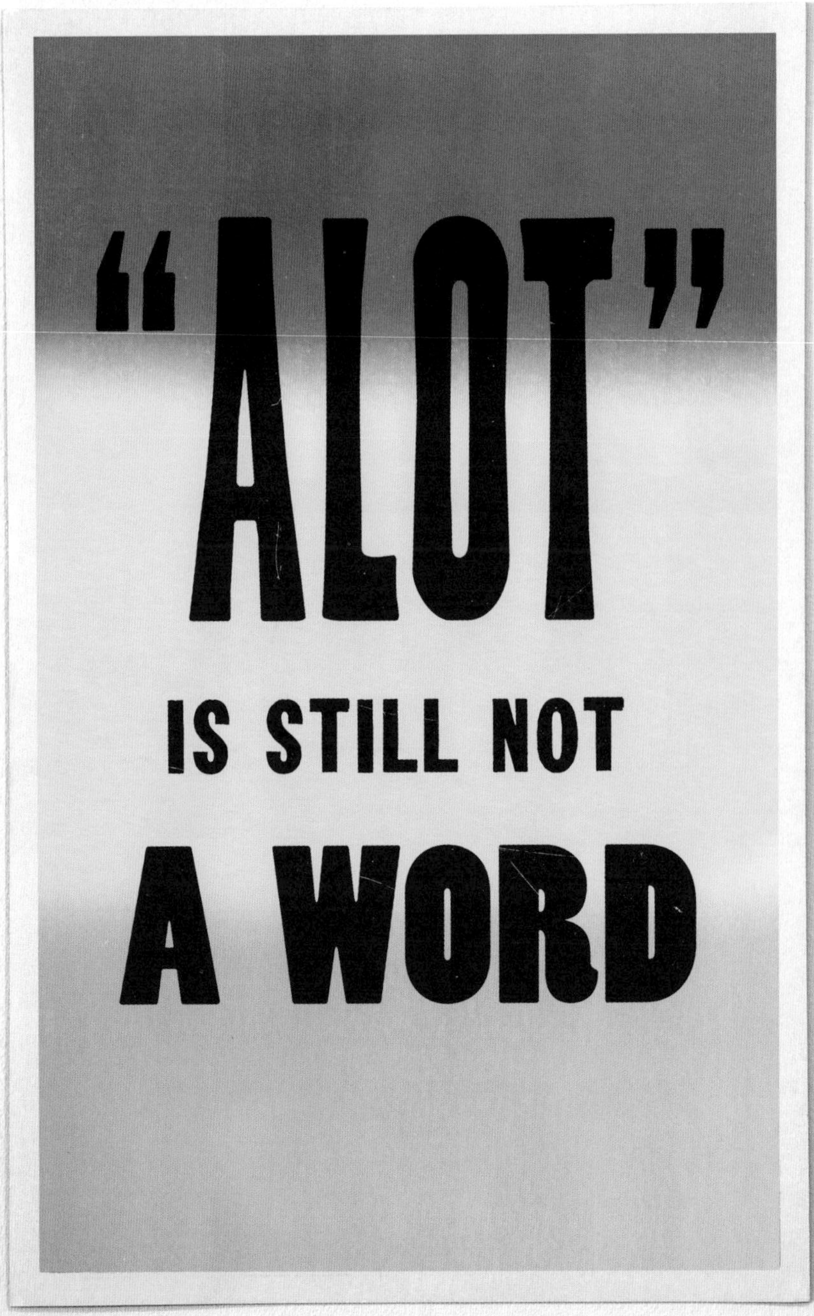
"ALOT"
IS STILL NOT
A WORD

№ 18

It shall be noted that, for all practical purposes, virgins and coders are synonymous. And the moment the coder discovers the pleasures of sex is the moment sitting in a dimly lit room wearing headphones seems that much less exciting.

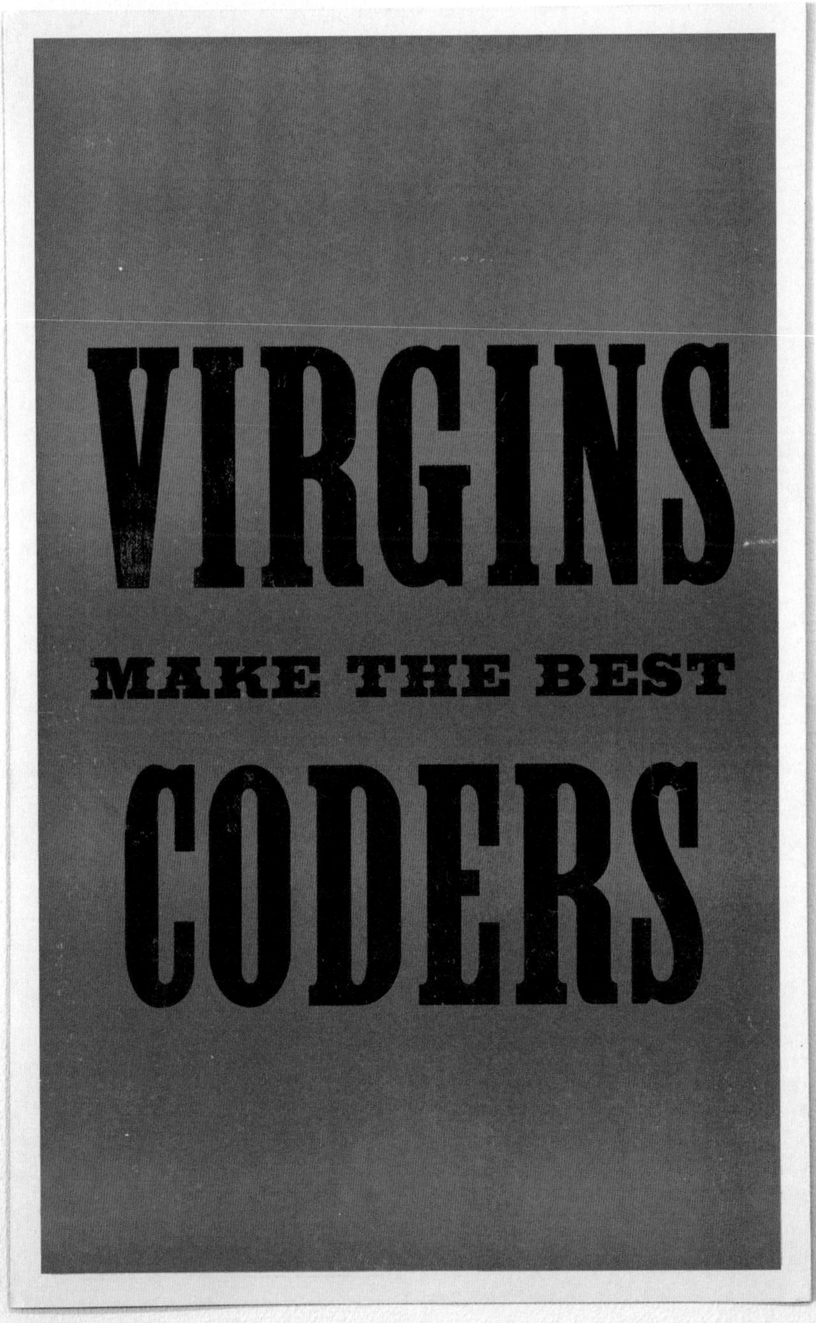
VIRGINS
MAKE THE BEST
CODERS

Nº 19

Employees should remember that anything they really enjoyed in college is an HR violation. While many workplaces resemble college dorms, they are not.

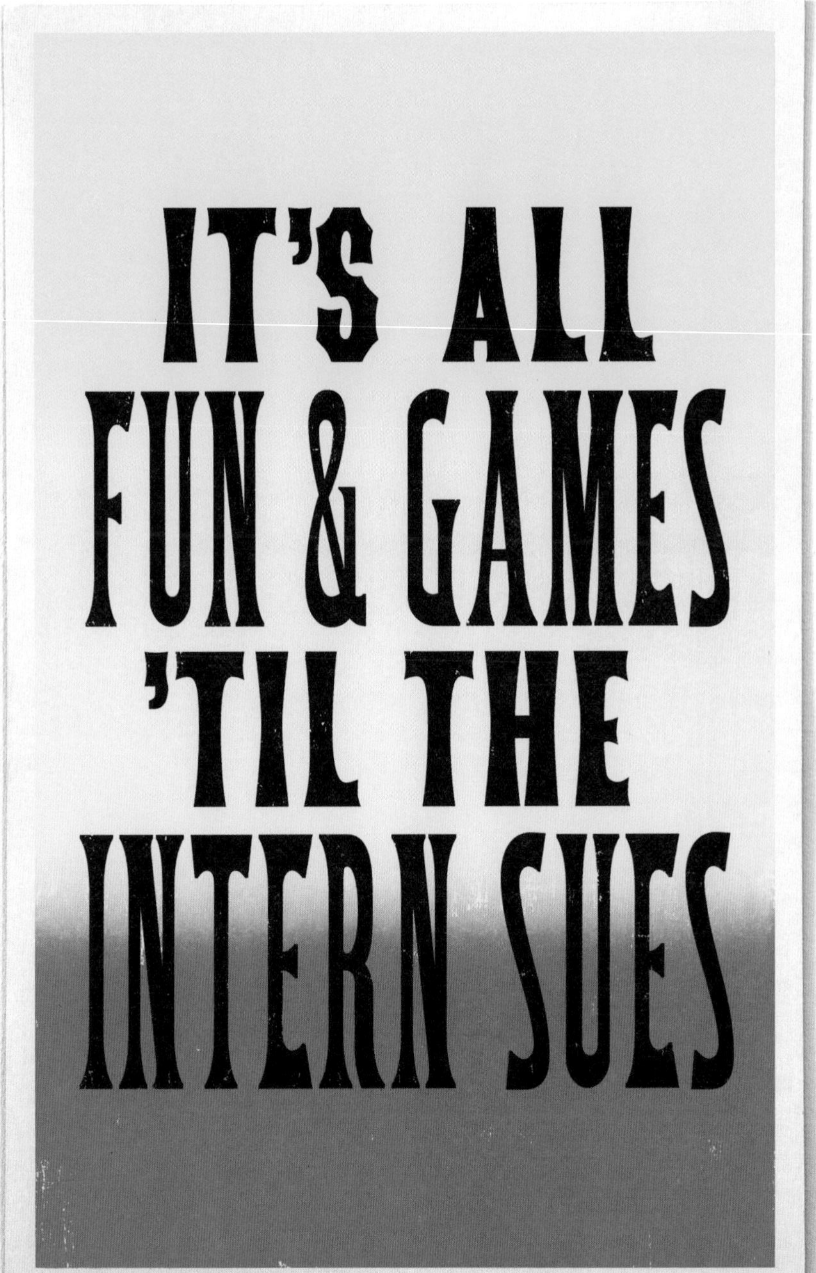
IT'S ALL
FUN & GAMES
'TIL THE
INTERN SUES

Nº 20

No office or workplace should provide a beverage that doesn't enhance productivity while, at the same time, making people's breath smell like rotting vegetables.

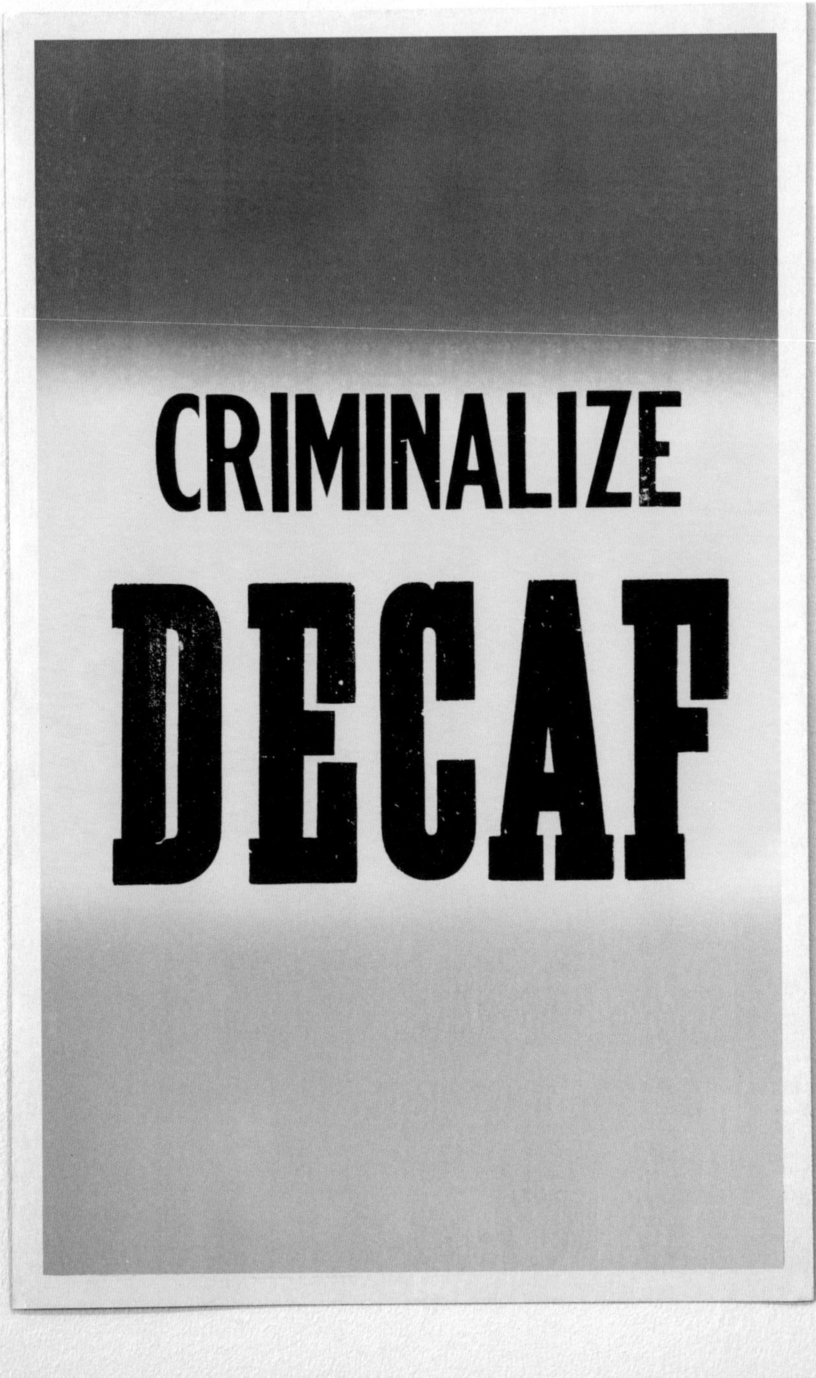
CRIMINALIZE
DECAF

MARRIAGE VOWS

ARE STILL VALID

DURING COMPANY PARTIES

MORALS AND THE WORKPLACE

OR,

IT'S ONLY DEBT IF SOMEONE COMES TO COLLECT.

Morality in the workplace has been an issue since pimply-faced kids first got their hands on the cash register and men have had secretaries and Napoleon complexes.

Watching *Mad Men* makes you wonder how anyone got any work done at all back in the day between the flirting, cigarettes, and multiple martini lunches.

Startups have managed to turn the modern office into a combination fraternity/sorority fueled by late nights, Red Bull, and stock options. (All of which, actually, sounds pretty good to us here at Division of Labor. Just saying.)

Workers often giggle their way through the sexual harassment training sessions and then respond to a coworker's crass joke by squealing, "Dark Hallway! Un-Wanted!" and then fall all over laughing as if someone added a bit too much Everclear to the punch.

There's the great story about the newly hired executive that crashed the company server because the quantity of porn he was trying to store was too large.

And we certainly know that expense reports and time sheets are often exercises in creative writing as much as they are documents for the finance department.

Think about this: Every September, office supply costs skyrocket at companies across the country because so many people think the office supply room is their personal Back to School shopping center.

But for most workers, moral questions in the workplace are the same as moral questions in life. And in the end, if you wouldn't want your spouse to find out about it, don't do it. If it'll make your kids think you're creepy, don't do it. And if it's gonna end with a grainy photo of you posted on Facebook and your name being used as the punch line of a joke about farm animals, don't do it.

Some of us are secure enough with our height and competency that we don't have to steal our coworkers' ideas and claim them as our own. While some of us can't come to terms with our insecurity and try to shag the paralegal and take credit for all her work while she's in the shower. What can you do? Just remember that whatever line of work you're in, the industry gets a whole lot smaller once HR finds out about what you did in Phoenix at last month's conference.

Nº 22

Hybrid-driving employees are expected to follow the same code of conduct as other employees. Possession of a high-mileage vehicle does not earn you the right to berate interns, throw tantrums, or steal egg salad sandwiches from the company fridge.

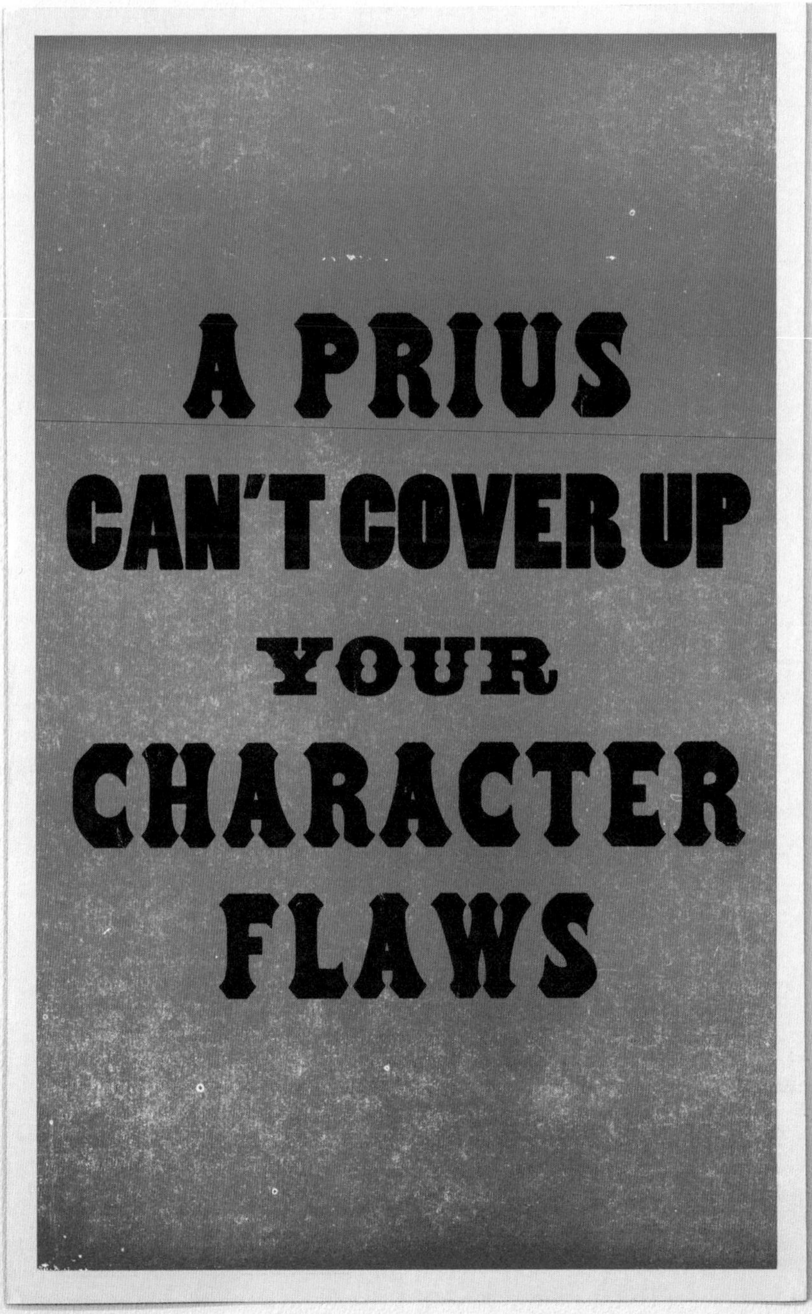
A PRIUS
CAN'T COVER UP
YOUR
CHARACTER
FLAWS

№ 23

All workers shall recognize that one person's comedy is another person's grounds for a lawsuit. People like suing each other. People with little sense of humor like suing even more.

IF IT'S REALLY FUNNY IT'S PROBABLY HARASSMENT

IF YOU DON'T HAVE AN IDEA

AT LEAST HAVE AN OPINION

Before tweeting, workers should think about conversations they've had with senior citizens. If anything you tweet sounds like topics discussed in retirement homes, i.e., what you're eating, how you felt when you woke up, or what you bought at the mall, don't tweet it.

STOP TWEETING BORING SHIT

№ 26

You can't "plus it up," "flesh it out," or "run it up the flagpole" —unless you work at the bottom of the flagpole and your boss works up top.

YOU CANNOT SAY "MAKE IT CRISPER" UNLESS YOU WORK AT PIZZA HUT

Employees wearing pleated khakis should endeavor to be more talented, more charming, and more productive than flat-front khaki-wearing employees. This can help counteract the effect pleats have on a person's ability to command a room, make a point, or be taken seriously, in general.

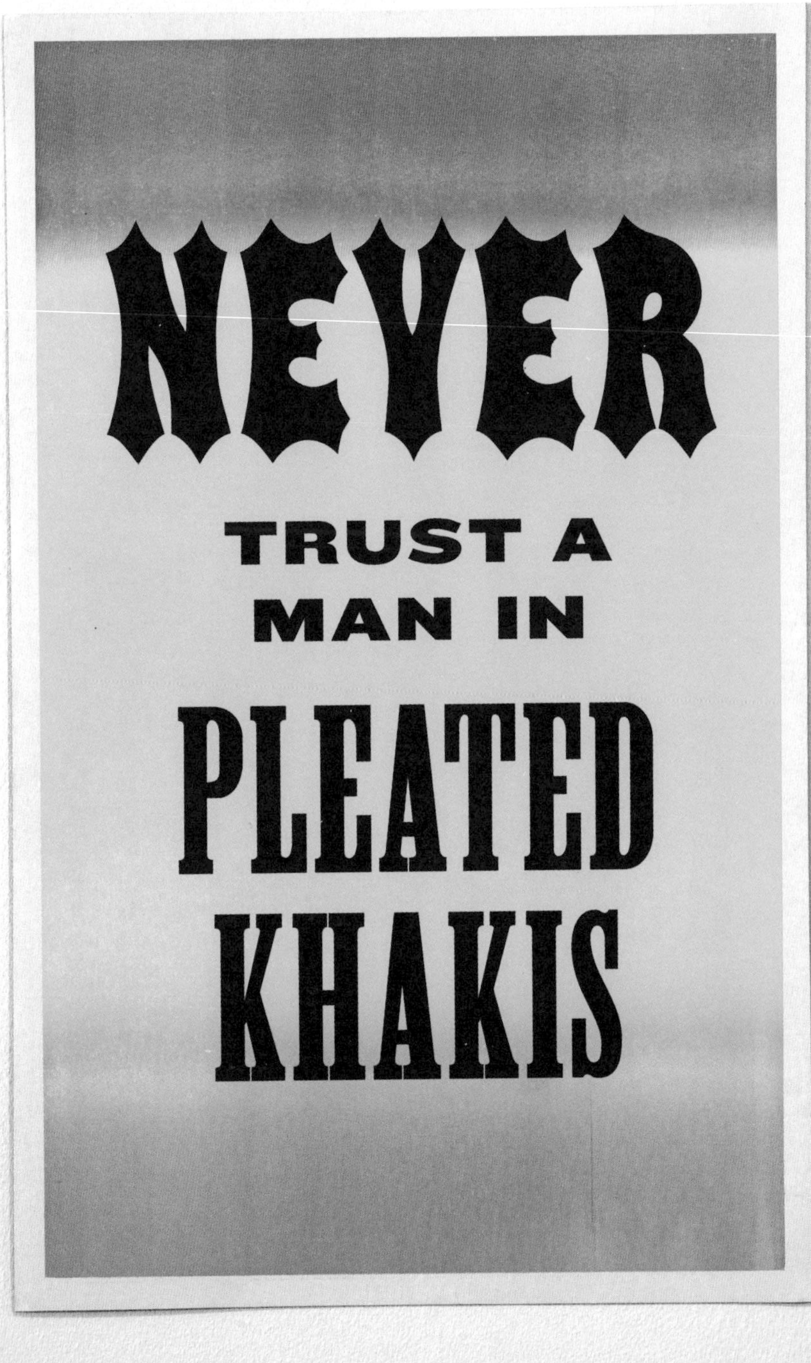
NEVER
TRUST A
MAN IN
PLEATED
KHAKIS

CHART

IF IT'S IN A

IT MUST BE TRUE

COWORKERS AND THE WORKPLACE

OR,

FOR GOD'S SAKE, STOP EATING TUNA FISH AT YOUR DESK.

Our coworkers are kinda like our families. We didn't choose each other, but we're stuck with each other. You have to treat your coworkers with the same tact you employ when you want to tell your self-centered, pill popping sister-in-law what you really think of her new hooker shoes (but you're wise enough to squeal, "Soooo cute! Where did you get those?" while swallowing bile). When your managing director comes in Monday morning and says, "That new Tom Cruise movie *Rock of Ages* was great! Maybe his best picture yet." Your response is most certainly not, "Are you on lithium, Dave? I could barely get through the flippin' trailer!" Because being right never got anybody anywhere in corporate America. Your boss doesn't want to know what you think. And your coworkers want you to fail so they can have all your accounts and the cubicle near the printer.

Total tangent here, but an important point: rotten breath has ruined more careers than rotten accounting procedures. Buy some mints. They're cheap.

The modern office has changed, but people haven't. The same character types that exist today existed fifty years ago.

- Suck-up
- Yes Man
- Bitter grumbler
- The boss's kid
- Deranged genius
- Super smart, equally ugly
- Loud talker
- Excessive sweater
- Secretary conqueror
- Rambling question-asker
- Brilliant new girl making everyone look bad
- Hot guy with shit for brains
- Tuna fish sandwich-eater
- Dude with amazing hair
- Lady to stay far away from at the Christmas party

The list goes on but keep in mind, for every person that drives you insane, you drive someone else insane. We don't say that to be mean. We think you're awesome because you're reading our book and all. Just remember if you get whacked in the next round of layoffs, someone's gonna be toasting your demise and stealing your office chair.

Final point about your coworkers: know who to suck up to. There are a couple of people with whom you cannot possibly grovel enough. First, whoever books your travel. They control whether you fly in a middle seat with a three-hour layover in Atlanta or nonstop in an exit row. Kiss that person's ass. Second, your boss's assistant. A good word about you from the assistant is worth more than gold. Buy them gifts. Finally, the IT guys. They can track everywhere you've been online and read every email you've sent— or make it all disappear. Think about that around the holidays. Probably worth more than a Best Buy gift card.

Nº **29**

Employees with Australian, South African, and Icelandic accents also sound proportionally smarter than their American counterparts. Sadly this rule does not apply to the Irish—their accent just makes them sound intoxicated.

BRITISH ACCENTS
SOUND
30 PERCENT
SMARTER

IF IT DOESN'T
HAVE A
MEETING
INVITE

IT DIDN'T HAPPEN

№ **31**

Parking spaces are taxable benefits, not a comment on how talented you are. Workers with parking spaces should not feel a sense of superiority or security. Because, actually, you getting fired doesn't just free up cash, it frees up a space for someone else.

DON'T CONFUSE
HAVING A

PARKING
SPACE

WITH HAVING

TALENT

Nº 32

Muslims, Jews, Catholics, African Americans, Asians, Christians, Latinos, homosexuals, heterosexuals, PETA, the elderly, liberals, conservatives, the Tea Party, the NRA, the NAACP, smelly hippies, trailer-trash, the Amish, private militias, people with plates in their heads, colostomy bags, or chronic foot odor—anyone on this list might be offended they were mentioned. But someone left off this list may be offended they were omitted. That's the way it is. If you have a point of view, you're gonna offend someone. But if you don't, no one's ever gonna know you exist.

IF YOU'RE NOT **OFFENDING SOMEONE** YOU'RE **BORING EVERYONE**

№ **33**

Workers "rolling up sleeves" or "putting noses to grindstones" should note that those notions have been replaced by Wellbutrin, Celexa, Lexapro, Prozac, Paxil, Zoloft, Cymbalta, and other pharmaceutical equivalents.

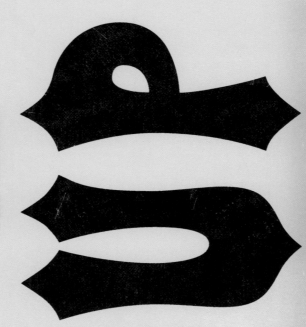

WHEN THE GOING GETS TOUGH THE TOUGH UP THEIR MEDS

NEW IDEAS

THERE ARE

NO

JUST REALLY CLEVER THIEVES

SHIT WE DIDN'T MAKE UP

OR,

AN ACTUAL SURVEY OF 850 OFFICE WORKERS AROUND THE COUNTRY

In order to back up our random thoughts and observations with actual facts and insight about the modern workplace, we commissioned a study with 850 office workers across the country. The survey contained questions about workers' behavior at the office and general thoughts about the workplace.

Wait, you guys did actual research for this book, you ask? Yes. Yes, we did. We not only did a proper survey to get a deeper understanding of human workplace behavior, we took the opportunity to ask a whole bunch of really embarrassing, mildly inappropriate questions that people answered quite graciously. Probably because the survey was anonymous and they knew their boss would never find out what they said.

We asked things like: How much time do you spend on social media at work? Do you steal stuff? Have you ever had sex in a company washroom with a coworker? Have you ever wanted to physically harm the people you work with? Do you know how to change the toner in the copy machine? Have you ever licked the handset of a coworker's phone in a blatant attempt to give said coworker some disease? Things like that.

We learned some pretty interesting facts about the lives of our fellow coworkers. Most steal, cheat, lie, or are in some other small way, deviant. Some hate close-talkers. More hate loud-talkers. And most do not share our personal disdain for pleated khakis. People waste tons of time on Facebook but do not want to see their coworkers on Facebook. Some cheat on their spouses with coworkers, but most don't. Some steal their coworkers tuna sandwiches from the fridge, but most don't want said sandwiches eaten in public areas. Some hang their kid's artwork in their cubes. And some think people who do that are stupid. (Probably people without kids or just really mean people with issues.)

Much of what we found out is, on the surface, trivial and sophomoric. But it gives us an interesting picture of how people behave at work. And since people spend well over ⅓ of their life at the office, that mindset pervades the majority of their waking hours. In other words, people do not necessarily behave as professionals simply because they spend time in a professional environment.

The survey was conducted by Dan Carlton and his team of consumer strategists at The PARAGRAPH Project so all the following facts are, indeed, facts. Hard to believe as some of them are. Enjoy.

NEARLY ⅔ OF WORKERS HAVE GOOGLED THEMSELVES.

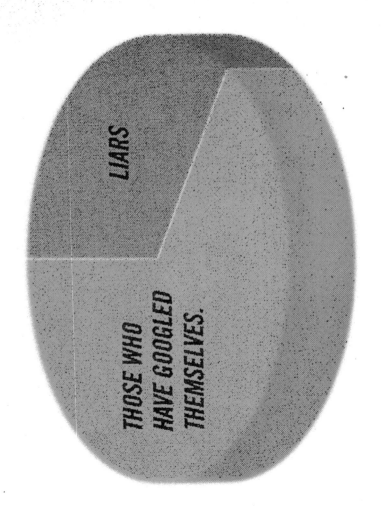

LIARS

THOSE WHO HAVE GOOGLED THEMSELVES.

19% of workers say "Googling themselves" sounds like masturbation.

71% OF WORKERS DO NOT WANT THEIR COWORKERS ON THEIR SOCIAL NETWORKS.

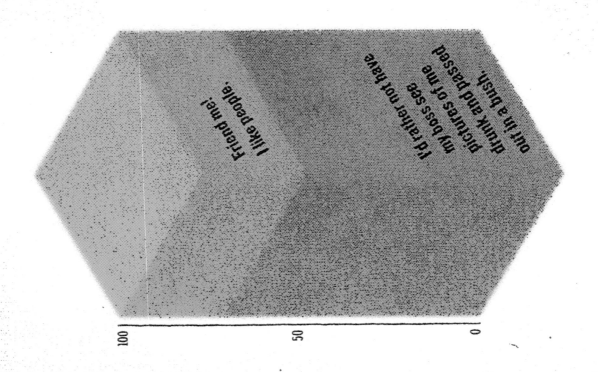

Friends and
I like people!

I'd rather not have
my boss see
pictures of me
drunk and passed
out in a bush.

100

50

0

40% OF WORKERS SAID THEY'D "GO CRAZY"

Can you make me
500 copies and pick
up some milk on
the way home?

IF THEY WORKED WITH THEIR SPOUSE.

No.

THE MOST VILE OFFICE SMELLS

(In no particular order.)

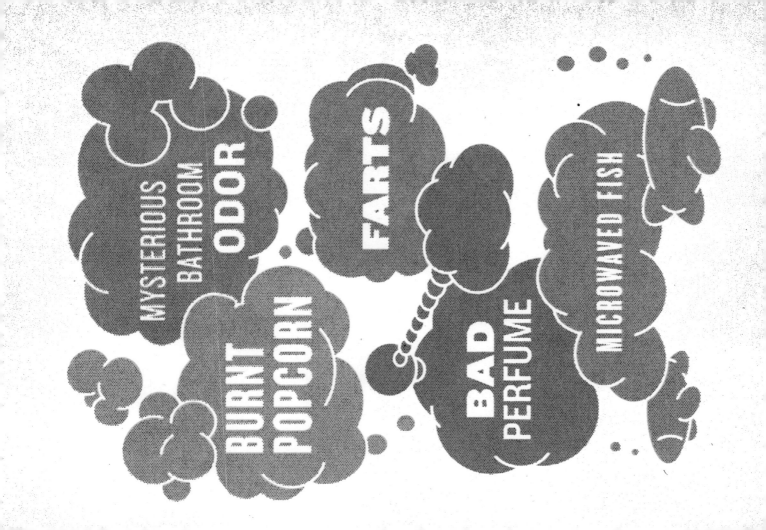

14% OF DEMOCRATS HAVE CHEATED ON THEIR SIGNIFICANT OTHER WITH A COWORKER.

33% OF REPUBLICANS HAVE STOLEN OFFICE SUPPLIES.

THIEVES

Proof that we're all dishonest, just in different ways.

13% OF WORKERS SAY THEY WANTED TO PHYSICALLY HARM A COWORKER.

*THIS GUY IS ACTUALLY IN JAIL FOR ASSAULTING A COWORKER.

77% OF WORKERS WOULD RATHER HAVE A PAY RAISE THAN PROFIT SHARING.

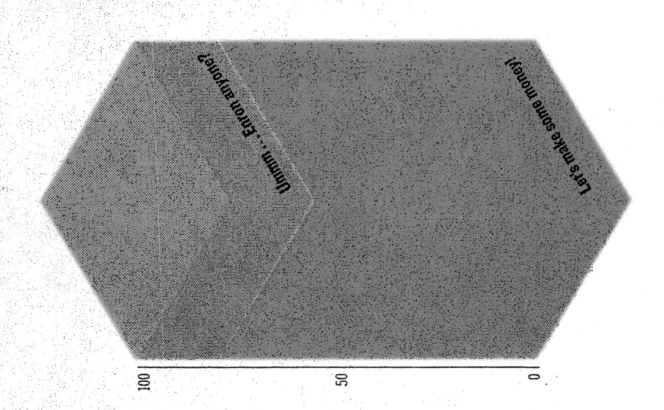

30% OF COWORKERS SAY "PLEATED KHAKIS" ARE THE MOST APPROPRIATE WORK ATTIRE COMPARED WITH **17%** WHO SAY "SUIT" AND **14%** WHO PREFER "ANYTHING CLEAN."

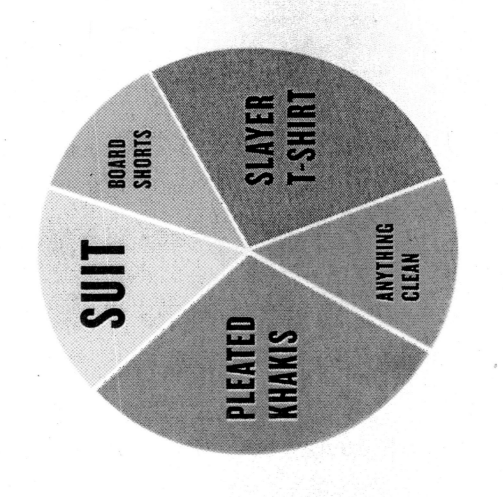

DEAR COWORKER

OR,

A FEW THOUGHTS TO SHARE WITH THOSE WHO WILL NEVER READ THIS BOOK.

Thanks for reading *Stop Tweeting Boring Sh*t*, or at least, thanks for picking up *Stop Tweeting Boring Sh*t* occasionally while you're on the toilet at the office. Not everyone you work with will read these rules. That is to say, not everyone you work with buys their reading material from that little table across from the checkout at Urban Outfitters. So you might have to help them out with their behavior at the office.

We've written a few notes to your coworkers and we encourage you to tear them out or copy them down and pass them along to those in your office. Or add your own insight to the constantly evolving Dear Coworker Tumblr Blog at dear-coworker.tumblr.com. Enjoy.

Dear Coworker:

PLEASE STOP SHOWING UP TO WORK REEKING OF PERFUME.

Smelling like a whorehouse is not attractive. Just because you have no olfactory system left doesn't mean the rest of us don't. If you need that much perfume, maybe what you really need is a shower.

Thanks!

Dear Coworker:

PLEASE STOP YELLING AT YOUR COMPUTER/COPIER/FAX MACHINE.

It's not the machine's fault that you don't know how it works. If we can all figure it out and you can't, it's your problem. So please shut the fuck up.

Thanks.

Dear Coworker:
PLEASE STOP SIGHING REALLY LOUDLY.

Things can't be that bad. If you think they are, imagine how loudly you'd sigh if you got fired and then couldn't get another job because everyone knew what a loud sigher you were!

Thanks!

Dear Coworker:
PLEASE STOP HANGING YOUR KID'S ARTWORK.

It's hard for me to take you seriously when your office looks like a grade school classroom. We know your child is proud of their work. But when my cat brings me dead birds that he's really proud of killing, I don't hang them on my wall.

Thank you.

Dear Coworker:

PLEASE STOP MAKING CONFERENCE CALLS ON SPEAKERPHONE FROM YOUR CUBICLE.

It's really disruptive to the rest of the office. Also, no one can fit in the cubicle with you, which just means you're on speakerphone trying to prove to others that you're busy. Which we get. Noted. You're busy. Now please shut your pie hole.

Thank you.

Dear Coworker:

PLEASE STOP WALKING THROUGH THE OFFICE ALL SWEATY IN BIKE CLOTHES.

Seeing men in Spandex is hard enough without seeing them ten minutes later in slacks still sweating.

Thanks!

THANK YOU

FOR

READING.

NOW GET THE HELL BACK TO WORK.

ABOUT THE AUTHORS

Author pages always make the authors sound like self-important douchebags. In this case those self-important douchebags are Paul Hirsch and Josh Denberg of Division of Labor. They have not written other books about the workplace but are officially considered experts on the subject from this day forward. Both would love to discuss their knowledge with Michael Krasny or Terry Gross on NPR someday.

ABOUT DIVISION OF LABOR

Division of Labor is not a government agency, so if your nanny is in the country illegally, we really don't care. Division of Labor is the ad agency and production company founded by the authors. This book is now the official HR manual for the company. More information at DivisionofLabor.com.

ACKNOWLEDGMENTS

Thanks to everyone at Chronicle Books for making this project a reality, especially Emily Haynes and Neil Egan. You guys are the best. Hopefully you all had as much fun with it as we did.

Thanks to Danielle Svetcov at Levine Greenberg, our agent who took a chance on "two bored ad guys" as you originally called us. You made everything happen and we appreciate it.

Thanks to The PARAGRAPH Project for the research used in this book, and thanks to Tribune Showprint for the original poster printing. You're both awesome.

Special thanks also to our beautiful wives Alison and Dawn and our wonderful children Ariel, Henry, Beatrix, and Theo. We do not share these wives and children, but didn't feel the need to get a whole lot more specific.